Milly, Molly
and
Special Friends

"We may look different but we feel the same."

It was one of those blustery summer days.
The clouds chased each other across the sky
and begged to be watched.

Milly and Molly lay on their backs in the long grass with their heads together. They were warm and thoughtful.

In fact, if Elizabeth and Poppy hadn't stumbled across them, they would probably have drifted off to sleep.

Tom and Jack joined in too.

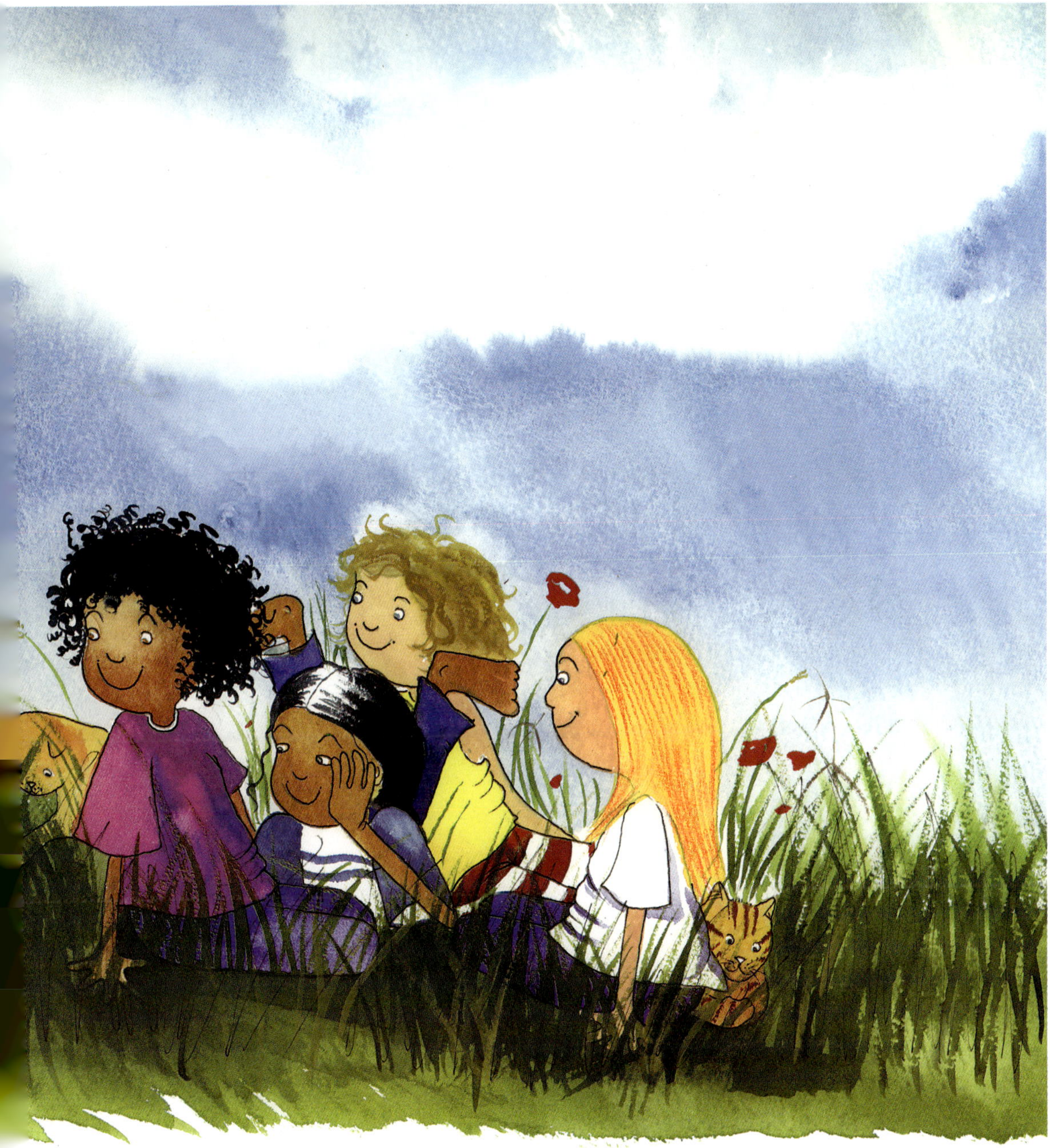

"This is one of my favourite things," said Molly.
"What is?" asked Jack.

"Lying in the grass watching the clouds," replied Molly.
"What's your favourite thing?"

"Hamburgers," said Jack.

"No Jack, not that sort of thing. Feeling things," said Molly.

"Like when Dad watches me play rugby?" suggested Jack.

"Yes," Molly said quietly.

"I like Gran's powdery smell when she reads me stories," said Elizabeth.

"I like it when Dad lets me reel in his fish," said Tom.

"And I like it on Monday when my sheets smell like sunshine," said Milly.

"I like sitting in Dad's chair when he gets up and the cushions are still warm," said Molly.

"And I like finding Mum in the strawberry patch when I get home from school," said Jack. "She always gives me the best ones."

"I like it when Dad puts a cold cloth above my eyebrows when I'm sick in bed," said Elizabeth.

"When there's thunder and lightning,"
Tom said, "I like getting into Mum and Dad's warm bed."

"I like it when Dad and I have hot chocolate by the fire and he tells me stories," said Milly.

"And I like smelling chocolate cake hot from the oven when I get home from school on Friday," said Molly.

Tom sat bolt upright. "It is Friday, Molly. Come on, what are we waiting for?"

"I'll race you," cried Jack.

"What a special bunch you are," said
Molly's mother.
"I like it when you say that," said Milly, around
a mouthful of chocolate cake.
And all the others nodded.